ESSENTIAL DK COMPUTERS

INTERNET

em@il

W9-AAC-723

ANNALISA MILNER

A Dorling Kindersley Book

Dorling Kindersley
LONDON, NEW YORK, DELHI, SYDNEY

Produced for Dorling Kindersley Limited by
Design Revolution, Queens Park Villa,
30 West Drive, Brighton, East Sussex BN2 2GE

EDITORIAL DIRECTOR Ian Whitelaw
SENIOR DESIGNER Andy Ashdown
EDITOR John Watson
DESIGNER Andrew Easton

MANAGING EDITOR Sharon Lucas
SENIOR MANAGING ART EDITOR Derek Coombes
DTP DESIGNER Sonia Charbonnier
PRODUCTION CONTROLLER Wendy Penn

First American Edition, 2000

2 4 6 8 10 9 7 5 3

Published in the United States by Dorling Kindersley Publishing, Inc.
95 Madison Avenue, New York, New York, 10016

A catalog record is available from the Library of Congress.

ISBN 0-7894-5533-1

Color reproduced by First Impressions, London
Printed in Italy by Graphicom

For our complete
catalog visit
www.dk.com

CONTENTS

E-COMMUNICATIONS

Communication has never been faster, simpler, or more universally accessible than it is with today's technology. This chapter presents an overview of electronic communications.

WHAT ARE ELECTRONIC COMMUNICATIONS?

When many people think of electronic communications they think of electronic mail, or "email." From being used almost exclusively in academic and government circles in the early 1990s, at the start of the millennium email is a household phenomenon, used all around the world and by all levels of society. But electronic communications encompass a broader spectrum of possibilities than just email. The television, the mobile telephone, and the computer all have a major part to play in our digital age, linked together by a huge global communications network. This page outlines some of the main components that are making electronic communications feasible.

Computers •
The computer is at the heart of the most popular means of electronic communication.

Advancing Technology
Technology is advancing at such a high rate that items bought today, such as computers, can become out of date within six months.

Mobile phone •
Mobile telephones can provide Internet access and receive email messages, as well as offering traditional telephone communications.

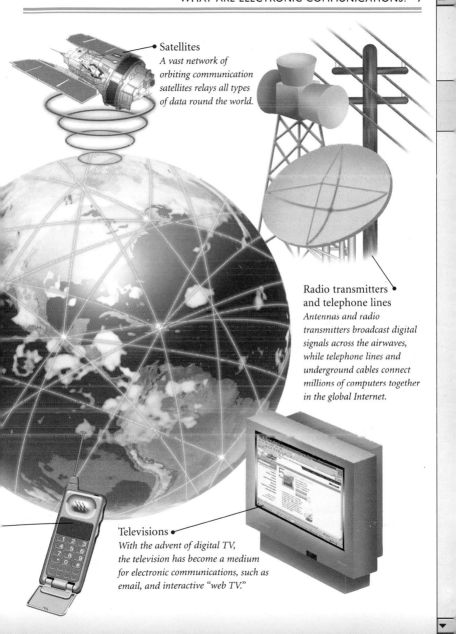

Satellites
A vast network of orbiting communication satellites relays all types of data round the world.

Radio transmitters and telephone lines
Antennas and radio transmitters broadcast digital signals across the airwaves, while telephone lines and underground cables connect millions of computers together in the global Internet.

Televisions
With the advent of digital TV, the television has become a medium for electronic communications, such as email, and interactive "web TV."

SENDING AN EMAIL

In order to send and receive email messages, you require several basic components: a computer, a modem, an account with an Internet Service Provider (this gives you access to the Internet), and email software such as Outlook Express. The illustration here explains what happens when you send an email.

THE EMAIL SYSTEM

The email system has much in common with the postal service. From your address you post mail to your ISP, which sends the mail via the worldwide network of servers to the recipient's post office (ISP), from which he or she can collect any mail addressed to them.

Servers
Your email passes through a series of these, which help to guide it to its final destination.

Sender's ISP
The Internet Service Provider acts as the doorway through which your email enters the Internet.

Your computer
The computer has email software that allows you to compose your message, address it, and send it via your Internet connection.

Telephone line

Modem
Your modem encodes the message as an analog signal and then sends it over the telephone lines to your service provider.

Screen
Your message and the settings in the email program are visible on screen.

Recipient's ISP
The message arrives at the recipient's service provider where it is stored in his or her individual mailbox. The message remains there until the next time that the recipient checks his or her mail.

Recipient's computer
The recipient uses email software to read and reply to the received message.

Telephone line
On checking for mail, the message is sent down the telephone line, is decoded back into digital form by the recipient's modem, and is received.

Global
communication lines

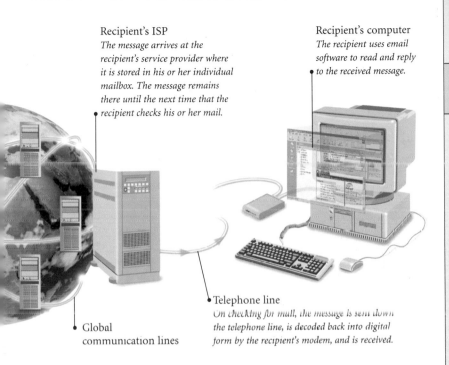

THE ELEMENTS THAT MAKE UP AN EMAIL ADDRESS

anna@merlin.provider.co.uk

1 User Name
Identifies the addressee.
2 Separator
An @ ("at") symbol separates the user and domain names.

3 Domain name
Is the computer address, with dots (periods) as separators.
4 Country code
All countries except the US use a

two-letter suffix as the last part of the address. For example, uk stands for the United Kingdom, il for Israel, and nz for New Zealand.

OUTLOOK EXPRESS

Outlook Express is part of Microsoft's Internet Explorer web browser suite of programs. It offers all the features you need to be able to send and receive electronic mail over the Internet.

WHAT OUTLOOK EXPRESS CAN DO

Outlook Express provides a gateway to the world of electronic mail. It allows you to send 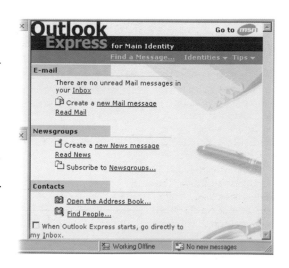 and receive electronic mail messages, and it provides facilities for you to record and store all your email addresses and personal contact details, in the form of an electronic address book .

Outlook Express has the additional benefit that if there are other people who wish to use your computer to receive their own email, you can create multiple user identities so that their email and contact details can be kept separately and privately from your own.

EMAIL

Email is the main activity provided by Outlook Express. It provides a user-friendly interface that makes it easy to compose, send, and receive email messages directly from the main window. Email messages can contain text, pictures, hypertext links to websites, and even self-contained file attachments.

NEWSGROUPS

For those who have mastered the art of sending email and want to branch out into the world of online debate and discussion, Outlook Express provides a newsreading facility that enables you to read and join in with electronic "newsgroups." Newsgroup discussions cover just about every topic under the sun, from world politics and all types of hobbies and leisure interests to more focused subjects, such as the life cycle of the dung beetle or sea turtle conservation.

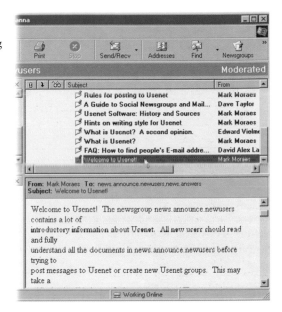

CONTACTS

Using the Outlook Express address book you can build up an electronic database of personal and business contacts. For each contact you can record name, home, business, personal, and other details. You can then use these address book records to address emails without having to retype the address each time. The address book helps you to manage your email sessions more efficiently.

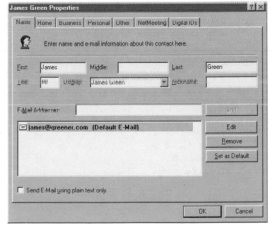

LAUNCHING OUTLOOK EXPRESS

Outlook Express can be started, or "launched" from either the Windows Start menu, directly from the desktop (if the Outlook Express shortcut has been placed on the desktop), or from within Microsoft's Internet Explorer program itself. Follow the steps to launch the program using any of these methods.

FROM THE DESKTOP

To launch Outlook Express from the desktop:
• Locate the Outlook Express shortcut icon. This has the appearance of an envelope with two blue arrows encircling it, and the words "Outlook Express" are written beneath it.
• Position the mouse pointer over the Outlook Express icon and double-click the left mouse button to launch the program.

FROM THE START MENU

To launch Outlook Express from the Start Menu:
• Click on the Start button.
• Move the mouse pointer up to Programs in the Start menu and the Programs submenu is displayed.
• Move the mouse pointer across to Outlook Express on the Programs submenu and click once. Outlook Express begins to run.

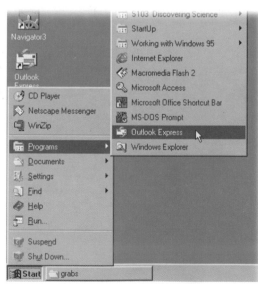

FROM INTERNET EXPLORER

When Internet Explorer is open, you can open Outlook Express directly from Explorer's Mail menu.

• Click on the Mail button on the main Internet Explorer toolbar.
• Select the option that you require from the drop-down menu.

• Outlook Express is launched, showing a new message window, or the Inbox, depending on the menu option you selected from the menu.

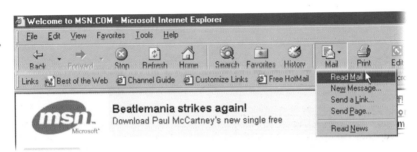

THE OUTLOOK EXPRESS PANEL

Once the program has started up, the Outlook Express window appears showing the Outlook Express panel on the left. This panel has shortcuts to some features of the program, such as creating new email messages and opening the Address Book.

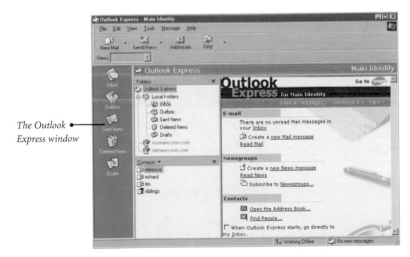

The Outlook Express window

THE OUTLOOK EXPRESS WINDOW

The Outlook Express window is divided into different sections, some of which are visible only when you perform actions they relate to. You can personalize the Outlook Express window to display as many or few of these sections as you wish.

WINDOW PANELS

1 Outlook Bar
The Outlook bar provides handy shortcuts to some of the key folders. You can customize the Outlook bar to include the folders that you use most frequently.

2 Contacts Panel
This panel displays a list of all the contacts that are stored in the current user's Address Book.

3 Folders Panel
A folder can be selected in this panel to become the currently active folder whose contents are displayed in the main area of the window.

4 Folders List
This shows all the folders and subfolders in which the current user's email and newsgroup messages have been saved and stored.

5 Views Bar
The views bar allows you to show or hide different categories of messages according to your choice.

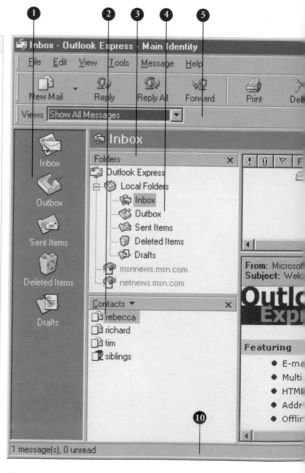

62 Using the contact panel

59 Reading messages by using views

THE MENU BAR

The Menu bar at the top of the screen, just below the Title bar, contains some menu options, such as File and Edit, that are shared with other Microsoft programs and may be familiar. However, the Message option, through which messages are controlled, is unique to Outlook Express.

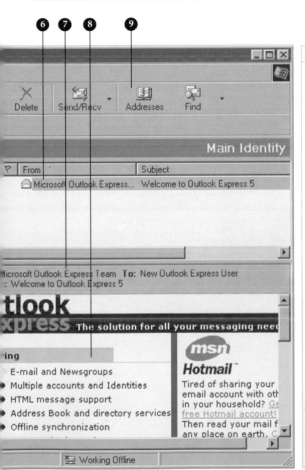

WINDOW PANELS

6 Message List
This shows a list of all the messages that are contained in the active folder (the folder that has been selected from the Folder list or Outlook bar).

7 Preview Panel Header
Contains summary information about the currently selected message.

8 Preview Panel
The contents of the selected message in the Message List can be read here.

9 Toolbar
The bar at the top of your screen displays buttons that enable you to access Outlook's main features quickly and easily. The items on the toolbar change depending on which part of the program you are using.

10 Status Bar
Displays information about activities that you perform and the status of your Internet connection.

16 | The Toolbar buttons

THE TOOLBAR

The toolbar for the Outlook Express window provides access to some of the main features of Outlook Express. You can initiate most of your sending and receiving from the toolbar and perform activities, such as printing and deleting messages, and searching for items in your mail folders. As you move from one folder to the next, the buttons on the toolbar change. For example, when you first launch Outlook Express only four buttons are on the toolbar, but when you go to the Inbox more appear. At times, some of the buttons appear grayed-out because that particular function is not available from that window at that time.

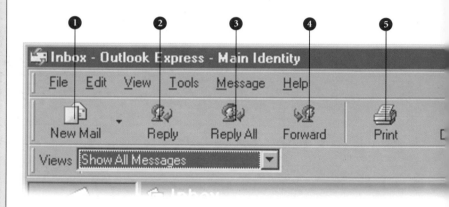

THE TOOLBAR BUTTONS

1 New Mail
This button opens a blank email message window. By clicking on the arrow to the right of this button, you can open a template containing a design – for a birthday or an invitation – in which you can type your message.

2 Reply
You can reply to any message in the Inbox by clicking on this button. A new message window opens with the address of the sender already filled in.

3 Reply All
By clicking on this button you can circulate a reply that is sent to both the sender and the other

recipients of a message in your Inbox. A new message window opens with the address of the sender and all the other recipients, including yourself, already filled in.

4 Forward
This duplicates any email message you have received in a message window, but leaves the

Sending
Emails — 32

Receiving
Emails — 46

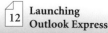
Launching
Outlook Express — 12

CUSTOMIZING THE TOOLBAR

To customize the toolbar click on the View menu, then on Layout, and then click Customize Toolbar. Toolbar buttons can be removed, or further ones can be added from the list of available buttons. The order of the buttons on the toolbar can be changed by clicking on the Move up or Move down buttons. The Text Options pull-down menu allows you to change the text, and the size of the icons can be changed by dropping down the Icon Options menu.

6 **7** **8** **9** **10**

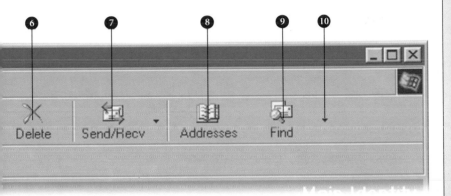

Main Identity

THE TOOLBAR BUTTONS

address field blank for you to forward the contents to someone else by typing a new address.

5 Print
Clicking this button prints a copy of the email message that you have selected.

6 Delete
Deletes the email message you have selected in the Message List.

7 Send/Receive
This sends any messages in the Outbox and checks for new mail.

8 Addresses
This opens the Address Book belonging to the current user and shows names and addresses, which can be selected.

9 Find
Opens a search dialog box so

that you can search for messages by criteria such as sender and recipient.

10 More Find Options
Clicking on the arrow to the right of the Find button drops down a menu containing further search options including searching for a particular sequence of words.

PERSONALIZING THE OUTLOOK EXPRESS WINDOW

Once you have become familiar with Outlook Express and know which features you find most useful, you may want to personalize the main window so that it shows only those panels and toolbars that you use on a day-to-day basis.

1 BEGINNING WITH THE VIEW MENU

This can be done from the View menu by following these instructions.

• Click the mouse on the View menu.

• Choose Layout from the drop-down menu that appears. The Window Layout Properties dialog box now opens.

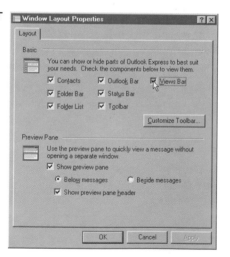

2 WINDOW LAYOUT PROPERTIES

Click the mouse in the various check boxes, in such a way that there are check marks beside all the items that you want to be displayed in the main window. Remove the check marks from items you do not want displayed.

• Click the OK button to save your new settings.

ONLINE AND OFFLINE WORKING

If you live in a country where you have to pay telephone charges each time you access the Internet, or if your service provider charges you according to how long you spend online (connected to the Internet), it will pay you to master the art of online and offline working at an early stage. It is perfectly feasible to do most of your electronic communication offline – that is, without being connected to your service provider. Composing, reading, and replying to messages can all be done offline. The only time you actually need to be connected to your service provider is when you want to send or receive communications, and this can usually be done in a matter of seconds. This section shows you how to move between online and offline modes and how to set up Outlook Express to reduce online time.

LAUNCHING OUTLOOK EXPRESS IN OFFLINE MODE

• Launch the Outlook Express program , but do not connect to your service provider first.
• In the Dial-up Connection box, click the Work Offline button with the mouse. Outlook Express will now open but you will not be connected to the Internet. You can now read and compose any email messages you wish without clocking up online time.

The Working Offline Icon

When you are working in Outlook Express, it is easy to check quickly whether or not you are offline by looking at the Status bar at the bottom of the screen, where the Working Offline icon will appear.

GOING ONLINE

After you have finished
working offline and are
ready to send and receive
messages, you can go
online manually (see
below) or automatically
(see opposite).

CONNECTING MANUALLY

Firstly connect to your
service provider in the
normal way.

● Now click on the File
icon in the Toolbar, and
from the pull-down menu
deselect Work Offline
(which should have a check
mark next to it) by clicking
it with the mouse. You are
now in online mode.

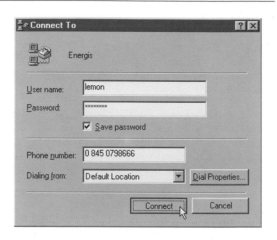

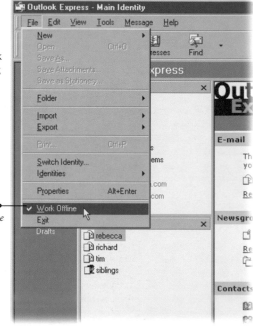

*Deselecting
working offline*

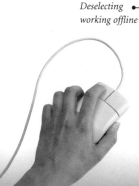

CONNECTING AUTOMATICALLY

Click on the Send/Recv button. This will prompt you to connect to your service provider.

● Click Yes, and then click Connect (unless your connection is automatic, in which case omit this step). Once the connection is made, messages in the Outbox will be sent immediately. Outlook Express also checks for new email messages and downloads them to your Inbox.

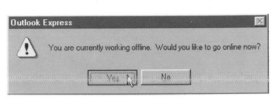

Connecting to the service provider

GOING OFFLINE

If you are online and you have some work that you can do offline, you can simply disconnect from your service provider in the usual way. However, there is an alternative.

Pull down the File menu and click on Work Offline. The menu closes and your online connection is broken automatically leaving the program running.

CONFIGURING EXPRESS TO REDUCE ONLINE TIME

You can set up Outlook Express so that it will automatically disconnect from your service provider after performing activities such as sending and receiving mail. This ensures that online time is kept to a minimum. To do this:

• Click on Tools in the Menu bar and then choose Options. The Options dialog box opens.

• Click on the Connection tab to bring it to the front and click in the check box next to Hang up after sending and receiving.

• Click the OK button to close the Options dialog box. Outlook Express now automatically disconnects from the Internet after sending or receiving your email messages.

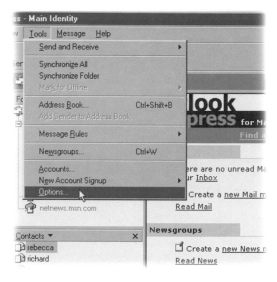

Check this box for automatic disconnection after sending and receiving

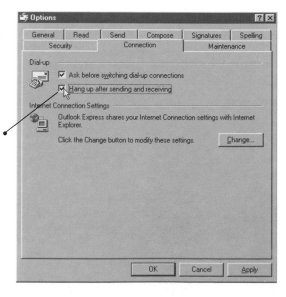

KEYBOARD SHORTCUTS

Throughout this book you will be shown how to carry out tasks in Outlook Express by using the Toolbar and the drop-down menus. However, many of the tasks can be accomplished using keyboard shortcuts. Unless you are used to using shortcuts in other programs, these keystroke combinations may seem clumsy at first, but you will soon find that they are quick and easy to use.

Select all messages .... Ctrl+A
Print selected message .... Ctrl+P
Send and receive mail .... Ctrl+M
Delete a mail message .... Del or Ctrl+D
Open or post a new message .... Ctrl+N
Open the Address Book .... Ctrl+⇧ Shift+B
Reply to the message author .... Ctrl+R
Forward a message .... Ctrl+F
Go to your Inbox .... Ctrl+I
Go to the next message in the list .... Ctrl+>
Go to the previous message in the list .... Ctrl+< or Ctrl+⇧ Shift+<
View properties of a selected message .... Alt+Enter↵
Go to next unread mail message .... Ctrl+U
Open a selected message .... Ctrl+O or Enter↵
Mark a message as read .... Ctrl+Enter↵
Move between Folders list, message list,
preview pane, and Contacts list .... Tab⇄
Close a message .... Esc
Find text F3
Find a message .... Ctrl+⇧ Shift+F
Switch among Edit, Source, and Preview tabs .... Ctrl+Tab⇄
Check spelling F7
Insert signature .... Ctrl+⇧ Shift+S
Send (post) a message .... Ctrl+Enter↵ or Alt+S

USER IDENTITIES

If you share an Internet connection with family or friends, you can configure Outlook Express with multiple user identities so that you can manage and store your email separately.

CREATING A NEW IDENTITY

Creating a new identity with Outlook Express is a fairly straightforward process. You can create identities that use one single Internet account, or identities that use different accounts. So, for example, if you have email accounts with two different service providers, you can configure identities to send and receive email from both accounts with Outlook Express. If you are setting up an identity to use a different Internet account from the main identity, you will need your account details available with information about your user name, password, email address, and mail server. Contact your service provider if you do not know this information. Once you are in possession of this information, follow these steps.

1 SETTING UP AN IDENTITY
• Click on the File menu in the Menu bar and move down to Identities. From the submenu that appears, choose Add New Identity.

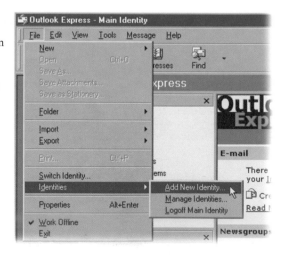

• Type the name for the new identity in the New Identity dialog box.

• If you would like the new identity to operate with a password, click the mouse in the Ask me for a password when I start box. The Enter Password dialog box opens.

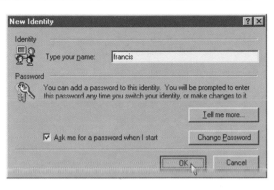

• You are asked to enter and confirm your password. Click the OK button when you have confirmed the password.

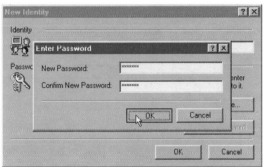

• The Identity Added dialog box appears asking if you want to switch to the new identity now. Click the Yes button to continue and complete the setup process. The Internet Connection Wizard now appears.

Selecting Yes completes the setup process

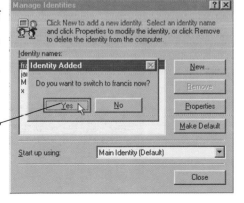

2 OLD OR NEW ACCOUNT?

• The Internet Connection Wizard takes you through a number of screens to connect you. A screen called Setting up Internet Mail appears that gives you the opportunity either to use an existing mail account or create a new account. If you would like to import the settings of another email program that you have installed, click the radio button next to Use an existing Internet mail account. If you choose this option, the Wizard asks you to confirm the settings, screen by screen, until you reach the Finish button.

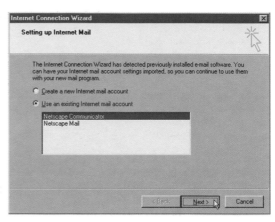

• To start a new account, click the radio button next to Create a new Internet mail account, then click the Next button.

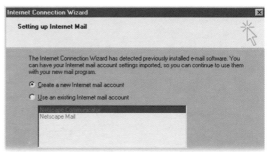

• Click the mouse in the Display name: field and type the name you would like other people to see when they receive messages from you. Click the Next button.

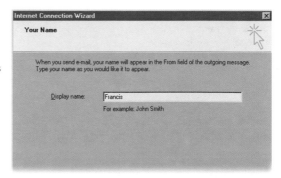

• Click the mouse in the E-mail address: field and type the email address for this identity. Click the Next button.

• From the My Incoming server menu select the type of incoming mail server for the account. Refer to your service provider for all this information.

• Click the mouse in the Incoming Mail Server field and type the name of your incoming mail server.

• Click the mouse in the Outgoing mail server field and type the name of your outgoing mail server, and click the Next button.

• Type your user name and password in the fields provided. These are the log on details you use to dial your service provider.

• Click the mouse in the Remember password: check box if you would like to log on automatically without being prompted for log on details each time.

• Click the Next button.

• To complete the creation of the new identity, click the Finish button.

• If you would like to import any contact or other details from other programs that may be installed on your computer, select the relevant options as they appear.

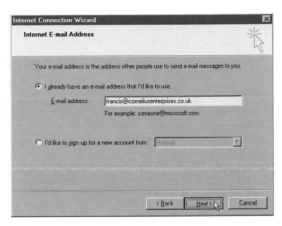

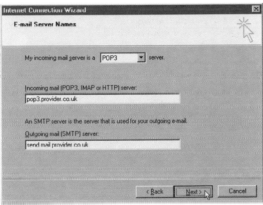

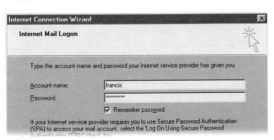

SWITCHING IDENTITIES

If you have more than one user identity, you can switch the current identity at any time without closing Outlook Express. This is done using Outlook's Switch Identities feature. You can access this from the main Outlook Express panel when the program starts, or at any time from the

File menu. When you switch identity, the messages shown in the Inbox and Outbox change, as well as the list of contacts. If you are online 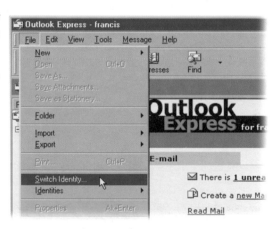 when you switch identities, and the new identity operates through a different dial-up connection, this connection will be changed too.

TO SWITCH IDENTITY

● Click on File in the Menu bar and choose Switch Identity. The Switch Identities dialog box opens.

● Click on the name of the identity you want to change to and then click on OK.
● Outlook Express closes briefly and then reopens with the settings for the new identity.

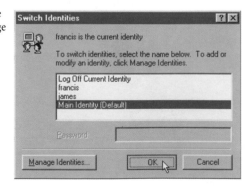

SETTING A STARTUP IDENTITY

If you would like Outlook Express always to open with the same identity you can elect to set up a Startup Identity using the Manage Identities dialog box. Follow these steps:

• Choose Identities from the File menu, then Manage Identities from the submenu.

• Click on the arrow to the right of the Startup using field to see the list of available identities.

• Drag the mouse pointer to the desired identity and click to select that option.

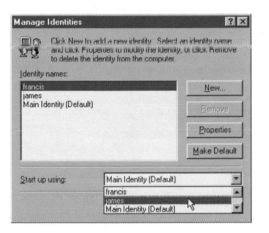

• The Start up using: field now contains the chosen Startup identity.

• Click the Close button.

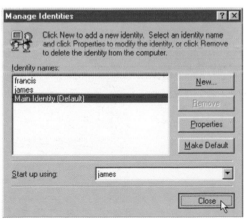

SETTING THE DEFAULT IDENTITY

To set an identity as the default identity, which will be the "active" identity whenever you launch Outlook Express, follow this sequence of steps.

● Click on the File menu and choose Identities, then Manage Identities from the submenu.

● In the Manage Identities dialog box click the mouse on the identity you want to be the default, then click on the Make Default button.

● Click the Close button to complete the process.

LOGGING OFF

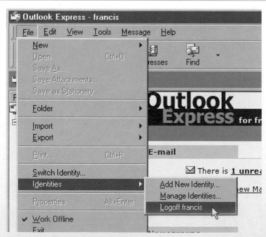

Once you have more than one identity in place, it is good practice to end your sessions using the Logoff feature. If you do not log off, the next time you use Outlook it will open using the identity that was in use when it was closed, even if this is not the identity that you specified as the Startup identity . You can log off by choosing Identities from the File menu, and then choosing Logoff from the submenu.

---

29 Setting a Startup identity

DELETING IDENTITIES
If you want to remove a
user identity, you can delete
it from the list of identities.
● Click on the File menu,
choose Identities, and then
choose Manage Identities
from the submenu.

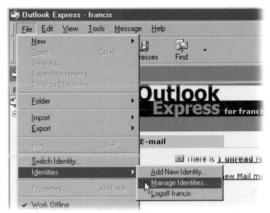

● In the Manage Identities
dialog box click the mouse
on the identity you want to
remove, then click the
Remove button. A Yes/No
box opens to ask you to
confirm the deletion.
● Click on the Yes button.

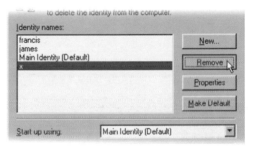

● You will now see that the
identity in question has
been removed from the list.
● Click the Close button.

Revised list of identities ●

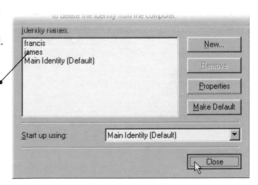

SENDING EMAILS

Composing and sending email messages is a simple process that uses basic word-processing skills, and is probably one of the first activities you will want to try. This chapter shows you how.

THE MESSAGE WINDOW

Email messages are composed in the Message Window, which is accessed by clicking the New Mail button on the toolbar ⌐. An email message is made up of several parts. The message "header" contains the sender, the recipient(s), and the subject of the message. The message "body" contains the message itself. A message may also contain other elements such as file attachments ⌐. These pages show the message window and how to use it to compose an email.

THE MESSAGE WINDOW

1 The To: field
This contains the email address of the recipient of the message. Every message contains the address.

2 The Cc: field
This contains the email addresses of people to whom you would like to send "carbon copies" of the message.

3 The Subject: field
This contains the subject of the message. Filling in the subject is optional, but it is good practice to use a subject so that people can tell at a glance what your message is about.

4 Message Body
This is where you type the text of the message. It acts as a normal word-processing window.

5 Toolbar
This provides access to the main activities you will want to carry out when typing a message. There are buttons for editing text (cut, copy, and paste); for checking spelling; and for sending and prioritizing the message when it is finished.

6 Formatting Toolbar
This offers some of the standard word-processing features to enable you to align text, choose the font and style, manage paragraphs, and add bullet points. Formatting can only be applied to text that has been selected (by clicking and dragging the mouse). Not all email programs have the sophisticated word-processing features that Outlook Express contains. If you do not know which program the addressee has on their computer, it is advisable not to add complex formatting to your email message because their email program may not have the facilities to display it.

⌐ 16 **The Toolbar**

⌐ 35 **Adding attachments**

COMPOSING OFFLINE

You may be composing a message offline to be sent later, and possibly to reduce phone bills. When you save a message when working offline, the message is saved to the Outbox. When you have finished the message and go online, the message is sent automatically from the Outbox.

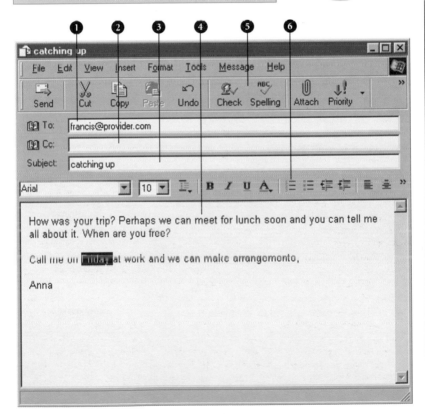

How was your trip? Perhaps we can meet for lunch soon and you can tell me all about it. When are you free?

Call me on Friday at work and we can make arrangements.

Anna

COMPOSING A MESSAGE

Composing a message can involve a number of different steps, which depend, for example, on whether you wish to include extra files, how many recipients there are, or whether you intend to send the message immediately. This section shows the basic process of composing an email and refers you to other sections where you will find information on how to carry out the other options.

COMPOSING A NEW MESSAGE

• Select a mail folder, such as the Inbox or Outbox, by clicking it in the Folder list or Folder bar.

• Click the New Mail button on the toolbar. This opens a new Outlook Express message window.

• Click the mouse in the message body area of the window and type the text of your message.

• Address the message.

• Add any file attachments you want to send with the message.

• Send the message.

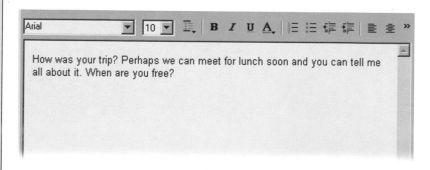

How was your trip? Perhaps we can meet for lunch soon and you can tell me all about it. When are you free?

| 35 Adding attachments | 38 Addressing a Message | 44 Sending Messages |

EMOTICONS

As your experience of sending and receiving email grows, you may notice in some messages that you read strange punctuation symbols. These are called "emoticons" (short for emotional icons) and they are used in email and other electronic communications to convey humor and emotion in a typed medium where it can be easy to misinterpret the intention and tone of what is being said. Emoticons resemble facial expressions when viewed with your head tilted to the left. Here are some of the more common emoticons and what they mean.

: -)	Happy	: - *	Kissing
. -))	Very happy	: - t	Angry
: - (	Sad	: - V	Shouting
: - ((	Very sad	: - O	Shocked
: - /	Undecided	: - {	Disapproving
: - p	Tongue-in-cheek	; -)	Winking

WORKING WITH
ATTACHMENTS AND FILES

As well as the text of an email message, you can also send files. These files are "attached" to your message. Attachments can include word-processing documents, images, sound or video files, and even computer programs. When you send an attachment, your computer copies the file and sends it with the message – the original stays on your computer. You can send more than one file with a message. Alternatively, you can insert the contents of the file into the message body itself. To add an attachment or insert the contents of a file into a message, follow these steps.

ADDING ATTACHMENTS

With a message window ⌐ open:
• Click on the Attach button on the toolbar.

• In the Insert Attachment dialog box, which is now open, navigate to the file you want to attach by double-clicking folders to open them.

• Click on the file you wish to attach so that it becomes highlighted and then click the Attach button.

• A new field appears in the mail header showing the name of the file(s) you have just attached.

Attached picture file •

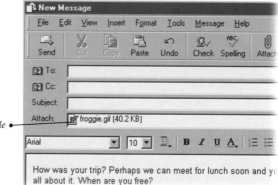

How was your trip? Perhaps we can meet for lunch soon and yo all about it. When are you free?

CHECK THE FILE SIZE AND TYPE

Sending large files as attachments increases the size of the message and the length of time it takes to download. Files over 500KB can take a significant time to download, particularly on a slow modem, so always check the size of a file you want to send. To do this, right-click the mouse on the file and select Properties from the pop-up menu. If you are attaching or inserting image files, try to use GIF or JPEG format files. These are the standard types of format for images on the Internet and nearly everyone can open them. They have a smaller file size than many other file formats.

INSERTING FILES

• To insert a file within the message, click in the message where you would like to insert the file and click on Insert in the Menu bar to select the desired file type, such as Picture.

• In the Picture dialog box, navigate to the file you want to insert and click so that it becomes highlighted, then click the Open button.

• You will see the contents of the file appear in the message body.

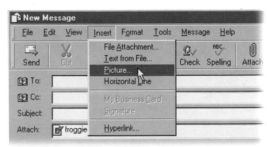

The name of the selected picture file ●

Picture file inserted ● *into the email*

ADDRESSING A MESSAGE

When you have composed a message and added any attachments, the final step before sending it is to add the email address of the recipient(s). Unlike ordinary letters, you can send a single electronic message simultaneously to as many people as you want by simply including all their email addresses in the address field. It is important when addressing a message to make sure that you spell and punctuate the address exactly. If any extra characters or spaces creep in, the message will not be delivered to its destination because the computer will not understand the address. This page shows how to address messages manually, by typing. It is also possible to address messages directly from the Address Book , but before you can do that you need to create records for your email contacts .

1 TYPING THE ADDRESS

• Position the mouse pointer in the Address field of the message window .
• Type the recipient's email address. There should be no spaces in the address, and follow capitalization and punctuation exactly.

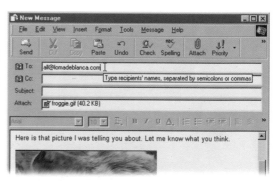

2 USING CARBON COPIES

• You can send a "carbon copy" of an email to one or more people at the same time as you send the original message by using the Cc: field in the message header. To send someone a carbon copy, click in the Cc: field and then type their email address.

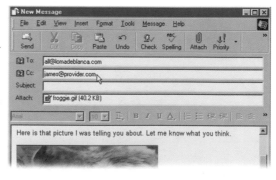

 34 Composing a new message

 60 The Address Book

 60 Creating Contacts

3 MULTIPLE RECIPIENTS

If you wish to include more than one email address in either the Address or the Cc field, you can do so easily:

• Click the mouse in the Address or Cc field.
• Type the first email address, taking care to replicate exactly the punctuation and spelling.

• Type a semicolon or a comma, then a space, and then the next email address. Repeat this step for each new address that you want to include.

SAVING A DRAFT

You can stop composing a message and save it to be completed at a later date in the same way that you can save any other computer file. Saved messages are known as "drafts."

• In the Message window click on File and choose Save.

• Your message is saved as a draft in the Drafts folder.

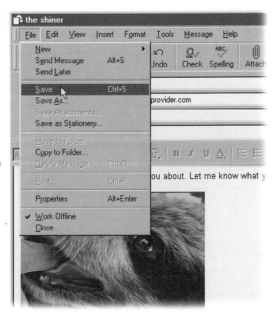

OPENING A DRAFT

When you want to continue writing a message you have saved in the drafts folder, you open it in a message window.

- In the Folders list click on the Drafts folder. A list of draft messages appears in the Message list .
- Double-click on the particular message you want to open. The message opens in a message window below the message list and enables you to continue writing the message.

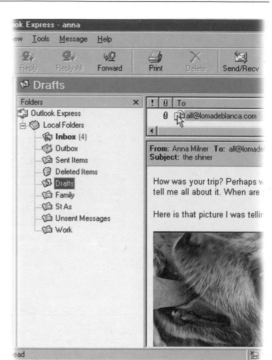

USING SIGNATURES

A signature file consists of a line or two of text that you can insert at the foot of an email message as a "signature." If you usually like to finish your messages in a particular way, perhaps including your name, job title, organization, or contact details, for example, signature files save you typing the same details every time you compose and finish a new message. To use a signature file, you type the information that you would like to appear at the bottom of the message in the Signature Options, and then configure Outlook Express to use signature files. It is also possible to insert text from a completely separate file for the signature. When you have followed either of the methods that follow for creating signature files, the signature will be added to all your outgoing messages.

CREATING A SIGNATURE

To create a signature:
• Open the Signature Options by clicking the Tools menu and selecting Options. The Options dialog box opens.
• Click the Signatures tab to bring it to the front and click the New button to create a new signature.

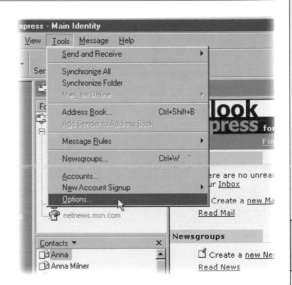

The Signatures tab ●

Other Signatures

If you set up a signature file, it will only be used for your identity ◻. When other people log on to Outlook Express using different identities, they can create their own signature files.

• A new signature appears in the Signature box.
• Click in the Edit Signature box and type the details that you want to include in the signature.
• Click in the Add Signatures to all outgoing messages check box and then click the OK button to finish.

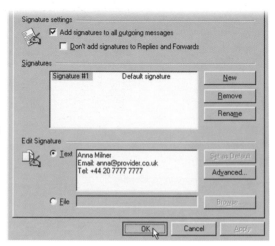

INSERTING A FILE AS A SIGNATURE

Alternatively, you may have a text file that contains a signature and other text that you frequently use to sign off. To insert this signature:

• In the Signatures tab dialog box, click the radio button next to File and click the Browse button.
• In the Open dialog box, find the file you want to use as a signature. Click to highlight it and then click the Open button. The Open dialog box closes.

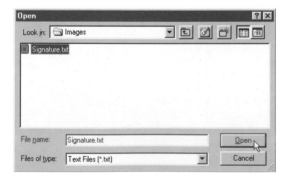

• The name of the signature file now appears in the File box. Click in the Add Signatures to all outgoing messages check box and then click OK to finish.

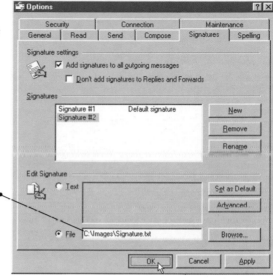

Selected signature file

DEACTIVATING A SIGNATURE FILE

If you have a signature file activated, you can deactivate it by changing the Signature options.

• Open the Signature options by clicking Tools in the Menu bar and selecting Options.

• Click the Signatures tab to bring it to the front.

• Click in the Add Signatures to all outgoing messages check box, so that there is no check mark in the box. Then click the OK button to finish.

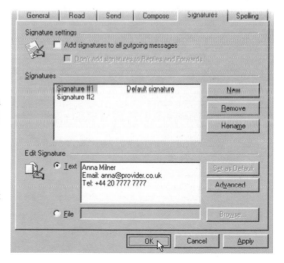

SENDING MESSAGES

Outlook Express offers several options when sending: you can send a message at once or send it later. For example, you can use Send Options to keep copies of messages, or to record automatically the addresses of people who write to you.

1 THE MESSAGE WINDOW

• To send a message you have finished composing, click the Send button on the toolbar. If you are online, it will be sent immediately. If you are offline, the message will be automatically stored in the Outbox ready for sending when you go online.

2 SENDING LATER

If you have finished a message, but do not want to send it immediately, you can store it to be sent later.
• Click on File in the Menu bar and select Send Later. The message is saved in the Outbox ready for sending when you go online to send your messages.

3 SENDING FROM MAIN WINDOW

• Click the Send/Recv button on the main toolbar ⬚. You are prompted to connect to your service provider. All messages that are in the Outbox are sent as soon as the connection has been made.

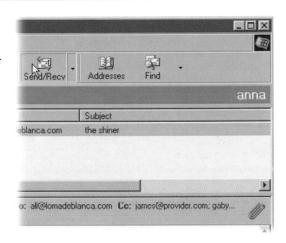

4 SETTING THE SEND OPTIONS

There are many choices you can make about how Outlook handles your email. In the Send Options dialog box you can personalize the settings. To select the available options:
• Open the Send options dialog box by clicking on Tools in the Menu bar and choosing Options.
• Click on the Send tab to bring it to the front. A list of sending options appears.
• Choose your preferred options by clicking in the check boxes so that there is a check mark next to the options you want to be active. Click the OK button to save your options.

RECEIVING EMAILS

Once you're familiar with Outlook Express and have sent your
first emails, you will be eager to receive replies. This chapter
tells you about receiving and managing incoming messages.

CHECKING FOR MAIL

When you launch 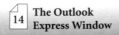 Outlook Express and
go online, among the first tasks the
program performs is checking your mail
server for incoming mail and
downloading new messages into your
Inbox so that you can read them.
However, you can check for new mail at
any time after that. This page shows you
how to check for and retrieve new
messages manually, and how to configure

Outlook Express to do this automatically.
There are several methods that you can
use to check for new mail. To try them
out, first open the Inbox by clicking the
Inbox button or folder in either the
Outlook bar or the Folders list 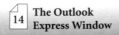. When
you want to receive mail you will need to
go online 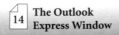. If you try to collect mail
while offline, you will be prompted to
connect to your service provider.

USING THE MENU

• Click on the Tools in the
Menu bar and choose Send
and Receive. From the
submenu that appears,
choose either Send and
Receive All or Receive All,
depending on whether or
not you wish to send
messages at the same time
as checking for new ones.

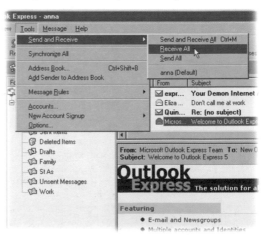

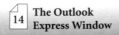

FROM THE TOOLBAR

• On the main toolbar, click the down arrow on the right-hand side of the Send/Recv button. A drop-down menu appears listing several receive options. Choose the desired option by clicking on it.

USING THE SEND/RECV BUTTON

• Click the Send/Recv button on the main toolbar. New messages appear in the message list and any mail waiting in your outbox is sent.

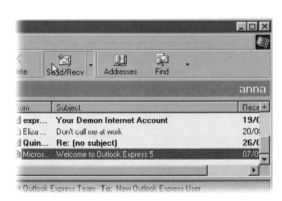

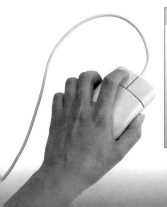

MESSAGE REQUEST

After performing any of the above methods for receiving new messages, Outlook Express will contact your mail server and request all the messages that are waiting in your mailbox. If there are messages waiting, Outlook Express will transfer them to your computer and store them in the Inbox folder; if there are no new messages Outlook Express will simply tell you so.

AUTOMATIC MAIL CHECKING

If you spend long periods of time online – surfing the Web, for example – you may want to configure Outlook Express to check automatically for incoming messages at periodic intervals. You can also ask it to alert you when you have new mail, by a dialog box or sound, for example. You can do this in the Outlook Express Options. These facilities will only operate when Outlook Express is running.

SETTING UP MAIL OPTIONS
• Click Tools on the Main menu and choose Options.
• In the Options dialog box, click on the General tab to bring it to the front. Move down to the Send / Receive Messages section and click in the check boxes to place a check mark against the options that you want to be active.
• To set how often Outlook Express checks the server for new mail, click on the up or down arrows in the minutes window until the required interval is shown.
• Click the OK button to finish and save the options.

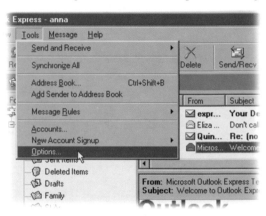

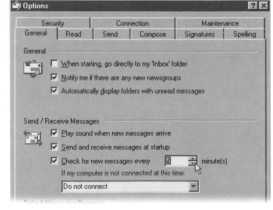

READING INCOMING MESSAGES

All your incoming email arrives by default in a message folder called the Inbox. The Inbox can be accessed either from the Outlook bar or the Folders list. It stores and lists all your incoming messages. You may notice that some messages in the Inbox appear in a bold typeface. These are new, or "unread," messages. When you want to read these messages all you have to do is to click the Inbox folder, then select the message you want to read in the message list. As usual, there are several ways in which you can read your incoming mail. To try them out, first open the Inbox by clicking on the Inbox icon on the Outlook bar.

1 OPENING A MESSAGE

• In the Inbox message list, choose which message you want to read and then double-click the message.
• Alternatively, you can select the message by clicking it once with the mouse, and then press the [Enter←] key to open the message. A message window opens displaying the contents of the message. If the message is too long to fit in the window, use the scroll bars at the side to scroll down through the text.

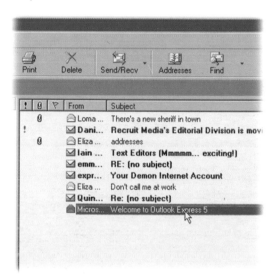

THE NEW MAIL ICON

It is easy to tell when new messages arrive because a New Mail icon appears on the Windows taskbar. This has the appearance of an envelope. To be able to view the messages, you must go to your Inbox in the main Outlook Express window ⬜.

2 READING OTHER MESSAGES

• If you have several new messages, you can read them all from the same message window using the Next and Previous buttons. Each time you click one of these buttons, the contents of the message window will change to show the next or previous message in the Message List.

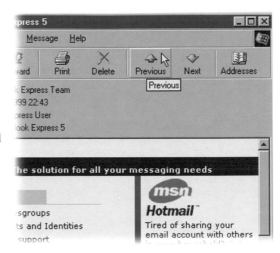

3 READING IN THE PREVIEW PANEL

If you have the Preview panel □ visible in the Outlook Express window ⌐, you can read the contents of your messages without opening a message window at all. Click on the message you want to read in the Message List to display its contents in the Preview panel. You can move up and down through the Message List by using the cursor keys on the keyboard to read successive messages.

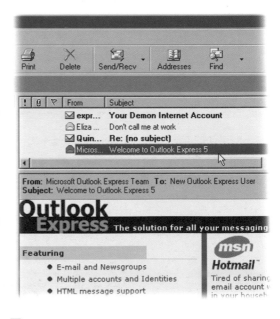

15 Window panels

14 The Outlook Express Window

READ AND UNREAD MESSAGES

New or unread messages are displayed in bold. Once you have read them they are listed in a regular typeface. There may be occasions when you would like a message to remain in bold – to remind you to act on it, for example. Or, you may want to mark an unread message as "read" – to ignore it, for example.

Outlook enables you to change the status of read and unread messages manually. To do this, right-click the mouse on the message and choose Mark as Read or Mark as Unread from the pop-up menu that appears. You can also find these commands as options in the Edit menu.

RESPONDING TO MESSAGES

There are several ways in which you may wish to respond to incoming email. You may want to reply to the sender directly, to all the recipients of the message, or to forward the message on to someone else, perhaps including a brief note of your own . You may want to print the message, or you may not want to respond at all, but just move the message to a new folder so that you can keep it for reference. Outlook provides for all of these eventualities. Many of these activities can be carried out from the message window. To practice them, first open the message.

1 REPLYING TO THE SENDER

• To reply to the sender, click the Reply button on the toolbar. A message window opens with the contents of the sender's message included, and his or her email address inserted in the To: field. Type your response and send it in the normal way.

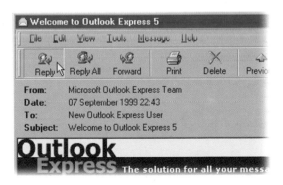

2 REPLYING TO ALL

• To reply to the sender of the message as well as all the other people to whom the message was circulated, click the Reply to All button on the toolbar. A message window will open with the contents of the sender's message included, and all the recipients' addresses listed in the address fields.

• Compose your response and then send it in the normal way.

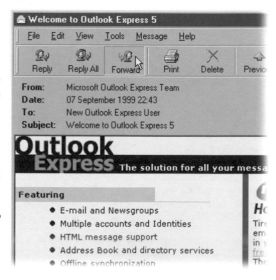

3 FORWARDING MESSAGES

• To forward a message to one or more people, click the Forward button on the toolbar. A message window will open with the contents of the sender's message included, but the address field will be blank.

• If you want to add remarks of your own, click the mouse at the top of the typing area and type your message in that area.

• Address the message to the recipients and send it in the usual way.

4 PRINTING THE MESSAGE

• To print the message, click the Print button on the toolbar. If the Print Properties dialog box appears, choose from the print options and then click the OK button.

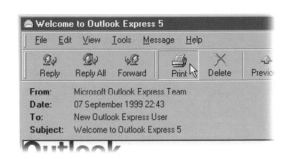

VIEWING ATTACHMENTS

Just as you can send files to other people as attachments □, you can also receive files with an email. A message that carries an attachment is displayed in the Message List □ with a paper clip icon next to it. You could be sent all sorts of files as attachments: image files, text files,

multimedia files, or computer programs. When you receive an attachment you have two choices: to save it as a file or to open it. To do either, first open the message in a message window □. All the attachments for that particular message are listed in the Attach field in the message header.

1 SELECTING ATTACHMENTS

• In the Message window, click on File in the Main menu and choose Save Attachments. A list of the attachments will appear in the Save Attachments dialog box.
• If there is more than one attachment, click the Select All button to select save the attached files.

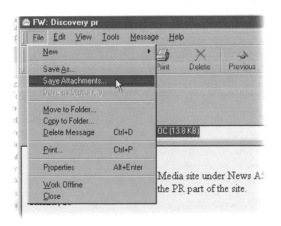

35	Adding attachments
15	Window Panels
32	The Message Window

2 SAVING ATTACHMENTS

• Click the Browse button with the mouse and navigate to the folder where you want to save the file(s), then click the OK button in the Browse for Folder box.
• Click the Save button in the Save Attachments dialog box to complete the process. The attachment is now saved in the folder that you selected.

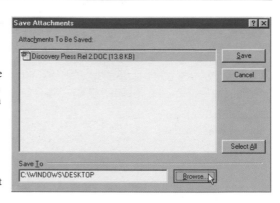

VIRUS CHECKERS

It is a wise precaution to check any attachments that you are sent for viruses before opening them. Many malicious viruses are distributed by email, often attaching themselves to messages without your knowledge. Be particularly wary of program files (these have a .exe file extension) that you are not expecting to receive. If you are in any doubt about the source of the file and its contents, use a virus checking program. There are many virus checking programs on the Internet that you can download without charge.

3 OPENING ATTACHMENTS

• To open an attachment directly from the message window, double-click the mouse on the file icon in the Attach field in the message header. The file will then open using the software needed to view it. If the computer does not have the necessary software an error message will appear telling you that the computer does not recognize the file or docs not have the required program to open it.

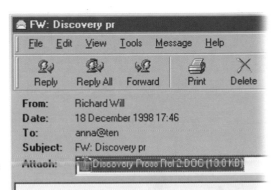

From: Richard Will
Date: 18 December 1998 17:46
To: anna@ten
Subject: FW: Discovery pr
Attach: Discovery Press Rel 2.DOC (13.0 KB)

Dear Anna,
Please could you put this on the Media site und
with the other Press Releases in the PR part of
Thanks, R.

FILE EXTENSIONS

When you want to open an attachment (even if you have saved it first), you will require the software that is capable of handling that particular type of file.

Usually it is possible to tell what type of file an attachment is from its extension. Some of the common file types you are likely to encounter are listed here.

File Extension	File Type	Software Required
.txt	Text document	Notepad, Word
.zip	Compressed file	Winzip
.xls	Spreadsheet	Excel
.exe	Program file	Runs itself
.doc	Word text file	Word
.pdf	Portable document file	Acrobat Reader
.jpg	JPEG image file	Photoshop, Paint Shop Pro
.gif	GIF image file	Explorer, Navigator
.tif	Tagged Image File	Photoshop, Paint Shop Pro
.psd	Photoshop image file	Photoshop, Paint Shop Pro

MANAGING YOUR EMAIL MESSAGES

There is more to email than just receiving and reading, and composing and sending messages. If you become an active email correspondent, before long your Inbox (and Sent Messages folder) will become so full as to be overflowing. Many people find it useful to create new mail folders into which they can move messages to be kept. Messages that you do not want have to be deleted on a regular basis to save valuable space on the hard disk. This section shows how to perform the basic activities that will help you manage your email messages effectively.

1 DELETING MESSAGES

To delete a message from the message list, click on the message file and then press the [Del] key on the keyboard or the Delete button on the toolbar. The message is removed from the message list and transferred to the Deleted Items folder.

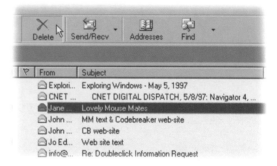

2 CREATING A NEW FOLDER

• Position the mouse on one of the folders in the Folders list ⌐ and right-click the mouse once. From the pop-up menu choose New Folder. The Create Folder dialog box opens.

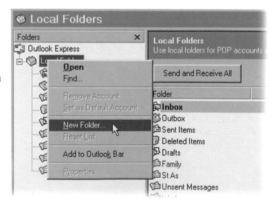

• Click the mouse in the Folder Name field and type the name of the folder.
• In the Folders list below click the mouse on the folder in which you would like to create the new folder. The folder becomes highlighted.
• Click the OK button to create the folder. The new folder will now appear in the Folders list.

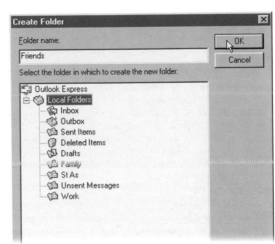

3 MOVING TO OTHER FOLDERS

• To move a message from one folder to another, ensure that the Folders list and the Message window are visible.
• Place the mouse pointer over the message you want to move and hold down the mouse button.
• Drag the mouse pointer until it is over the folder into which you would like to move the message. Release the mouse button and the message is relocated in the new folder.

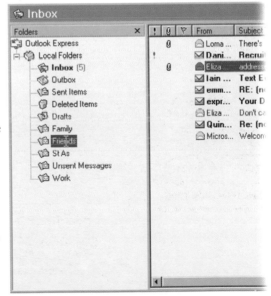

4 DELETING FOLDERS

To delete a folder from the Folders list:

• Click the mouse on the folder you want to delete so that it becomes highlighted.

• Press the [Del] key or the Delete button on the toolbar to delete the folder.

• Confirm the operation by clicking the Yes button. The folder is removed from the Folders list.

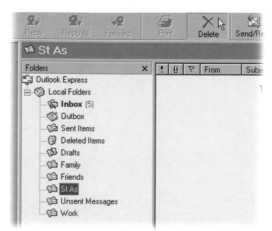

5 SAVING MESSAGES AS FILES

To save an email as a file that you can access from programs other than Outlook Express, open the message in a message window ⌐ and click the mouse on the File menu. Select Save As from the drop-down menu and then navigate to the folder where you want to save the file.

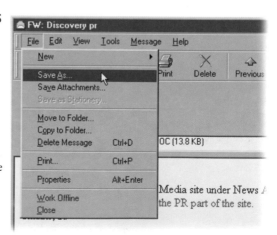

• Type the name of the file in the File name field and then click the Save button with the mouse to finish the process.

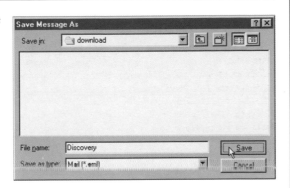

READING MESSAGES BY USING VIEWS

You can preselect how your messages are displayed.
• Click on View in the Menu bar and choose Current View. A submenu opens with several views. The main views have the following effect:
• Show all messages: All messages in one of your folders are displayed.
• Hide read messages: This view hides messages once you've read them.
• Hide read or ignored messages: This view hides read messages and those you have told Outlook Express to ignore.

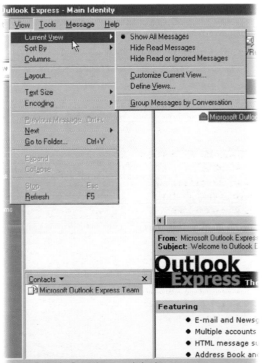

THE ADDRESS BOOK

**The Address Book offers features to record and store details of
your contacts. You can refer to these details when sending
emails, making addressing a simple point and click operation.**

CREATING CONTACTS

The Address Book offers a comprehensive
filing system for contact details, with fields
for home, business, family, and personal
details as well as the ability to record
important dates such as birthdays and
anniversaries. Outlook Express uses the
standard Windows Address Book (which
can be accessed directly from the
Windows Accessories menu) to store your

contact details. If you have already made
use of this feature in Windows, those
contact details will be readily available to
Outlook Express. To be of use within
Outlook Express, a contact record must
include the email address and name; all
other information is optional. These
instructions show the different ways in
which you can create new contacts.

FROM AN
OPEN MESSAGE

● Open a message 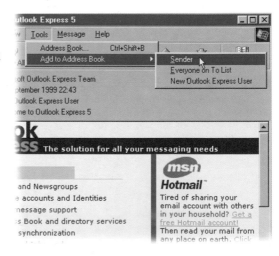 from
the person you want to add
to the Address Book.
● Click Tools in the Menu
bar and click on Add to
Address Book and choose
Sender from the submenu.

• The Address Book
properties box will open
showing the information
for the new contact.
• Click on OK and the
sender's name and email
address are added to your
address book.

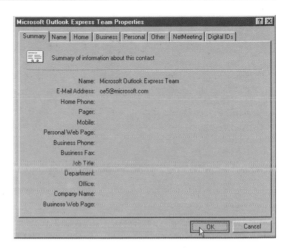

FROM THE INBOX

• If the Inbox is not already
open, click on Inbox in the
Folders list or Outlook bar.
• In the Message list, right
click the mouse on a
message from the person
you want to add to the
address book.
• Choose Add Sender to
Address Book from the
pop-up menu.
• The address is added
automatically to your
address book.

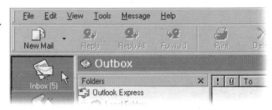

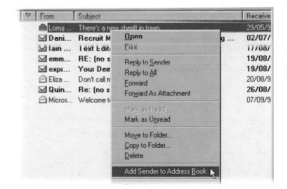

USING THE CONTACT PANEL

• This is the manual method for adding a new contact. With the Contact panel open in the Outlook Express Window □:

• In the Contact panel, click the Contacts button. Choose New Contact from the drop-down menu.

• In the Properties box, click in the E-mail Address field and type the person's email address.

• If they have more than one email address, click the Add button after you have typed each address.

• Complete any other fields that require an entry by clicking the mouse in the field and typing the entry.

• Click on the OK button when you have finished to save the contact details.

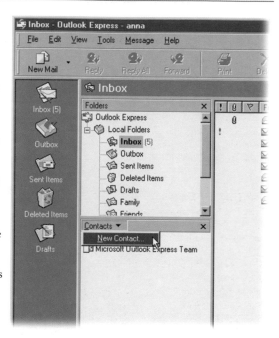

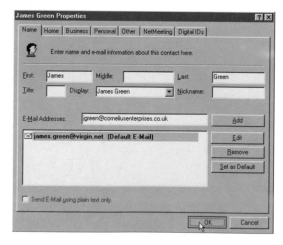

USING ADDRESS GROUPS

If you have a number of contacts to which you send emails collectively on a regular basis, you may want to create an address group. Creating an address group enables you to send a message to all its members simultaneously by specifying just the group address in the address field of the message window ▯. It saves you having to add each member's address individually to the email and ensures, particularly with large groups, that nobody gets missed out. To create an address group, follow the steps below.

1 MANUALLY USING ADDRESS BOOK

● Open the Address Book by clicking the Address button on the Menu bar. (You can also do this by clicking Tools and choosing Address Book.)
● On the Address Book toolbar, click the New button and choose New Contact from the menu.
● Now follow the instructions for manually adding a contact, as shown in Step 3 (opposite).

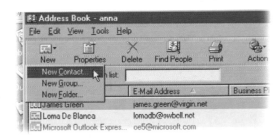

2 CREATING A NEW GROUP

● First, create and name a new group:
● Click the Address button to open the Address Book.
● On the Address Book toolbar, click the New button and choose New Group from the menu. The Properties box opens.

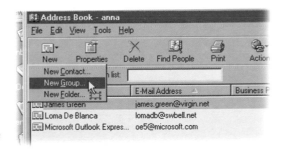

• Click the mouse in the Group Name: field and type the name of the group. This can be anything you choose and what you enter is shown in the title bar of the Properties box.

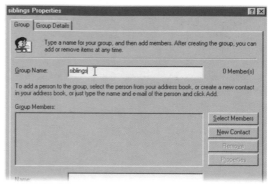

3 ADDING GROUP MEMBERS

• Once you have created the group itself, you must add members to it. These can be either existing contacts or people whose details have not yet been added to the Address Book.

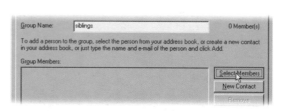

• To add an existing contact to the group click the Select Members button.
• Use the scroll bars to find the contact in the list, and then click on the name to highlight it.
• Now click on the Select button with the mouse to transfer that contact to the list of group members on the right.
• Repeat this process for each member of the group and then click on OK when you have finished.

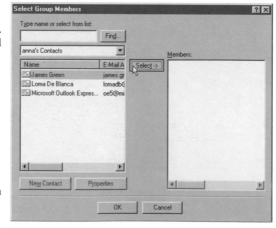

4 ADDING A NEW CONTACT

• Still in the group Properties box, click the New Contact button.

• Follow the steps above for adding group members.

• Repeat this process for each new contact you want to add to the group.

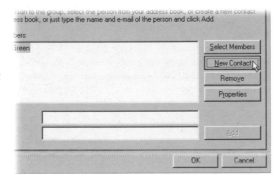

5 SAVING THE GROUP

• When you have added all the existing and new contacts to the group, finish and save your changes by clicking on OK. The group you have just created will now be listed in the address book. Groups are shown in bold typeface.

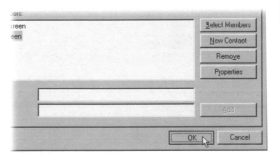

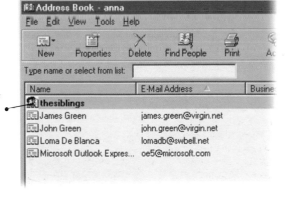

New group appears in the address book

EDITING AND DELETING CONTACTS

Once you have created your contacts and set up address groups, occasions will arise when you will want to change the details contained in your address book at some point. This may be either adding members of a group, removing members from a group, or deleting old contacts. This can done easily from Outlook Express, or even by opening the Address Book directly from the Windows Accessories menu.

1 EDITING GROUPS AND CONTACTS

• Click on the Address button on the main toolbar to open the Address Book.
• Click the mouse once on the contact or group whose details you wish to amend. The name will become highlighted.
• Click on the Properties button on the toolbar in the Address Book window to open the Properties box for that particular contact. You can now make any changes you want by clicking the tabs along the top to bring up the different pages, and then deleting old details and entering new ones in the relevant fields.
• When you have finished making the changes, click on OK to close the Properties box and to save the changes you have made.

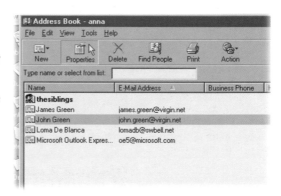

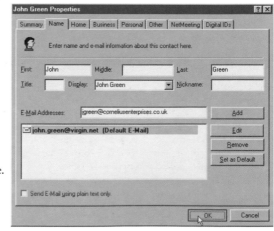

2 DELETING CONTACTS

● If you wish to delete a contact or an entire group, you can do this simply by using the right mouse button. Whether your contacts are listed in the Address Book (accessed from the Address button on the toolbar) or in the Contacts panel , you can delete them by following these steps:

● Right-click on the contact you want to delete.

● Choose Delete from the pop-up menu. The contact is now deleted from the list.

● Confirm the operation by clicking the Yes button.

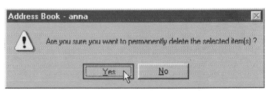

ORGANIZING YOUR ADDRESS BOOK

There are several ways to organize your address book to find contacts and groups easily. Sorting can be carried out alphabetically by first or last names, and by email address. Also the list can be arranged in either ascending or descending order. The order of the columns can also be changed, so that the more important information can be given prominence.

● To sort contacts by name, email address, or by phone number, click that particular heading at the top of the column.

● To toggle between ascending and descending order, click on the column heading.

● To change the order of the columns, hold down the mouse button over a heading and drag it to the required location and release the mouse button.

ADDRESSING MESSAGES

The Address Book stores all the email and group addresses that you set up and the features that it contains are designed to make the process of addressing your emails very simple. When you have composed your email and are ready to add the address(es) to which it is to be sent, you are just a few mouse clicks away from sending. To add an address that is stored in your address book to the message field of an email that is now ready to send, simply follow these steps.

1 FILLING IN THE ADDRESS FIELDS

• Click the mouse on the book icon next to the To: button in the message header. This opens the Select Recipient's dialog box and presents you with a list of all the contacts in the Address Book.
• In the left-hand panel, click on the name of the person who you want to send the message to. The name becomes highlighted.
• Click the To:-> button if you want to add that person or group to the list of message recipients.

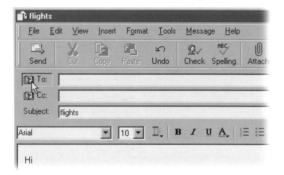

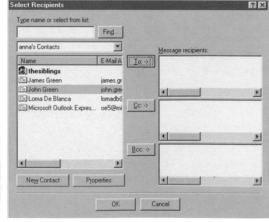

• Click the Cc:-> button if you want to add that person or group to the Carbon Copy field.

• Repeat these steps for each person or group that you want to send the message to.

• Click the OK button to finish addressing the message. You are now ready to send the message.

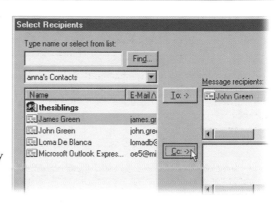

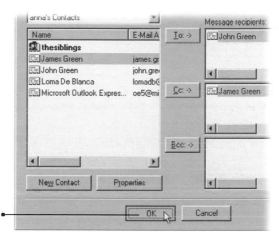

Click OK to finish entering recipient's names ●

Recipients appear in the Names field ●

GLOSSARY

ADDRESS BOOK
A central store for contact information for retrieving easily and simply.

ATTACHMENT
Almost any type of file can be sent within an email by "attaching" it to a message that you send.

CC: BOX
Text field where names can be inserted of people who are going to receive a "carbon copy" of the message.

DIRECTORY SERVICE
An extremely powerful search tool designed to help you find people and businesses worldwide.

DOWNLOAD
Transferring data from one computer to another. Your browser downloads HTML code and graphics to display a page.

**EMAIL
(ELECTRONIC MAIL)**
The system for sending electronic messages between computers.

EXCLAMATION ICON
This icon appears next to a message when the sender has attached a high priority to it.

IDENTITIES
Identities can be created in Outlook Express so that each person who uses Outlook Express on a computer can organize, send, and receive their own emails independently of other identities.

INBOX
This is the name of the folder in which Outlook Express stores incoming messages by default.

INTERNET
The network of interconnected computers that communicate using the TCP/IP protocol.

INTERNET SERVICE PROVIDER
A business that provides a connection to the Internet.

MAIL SERVER
A large computer used by service providers to relay email messages over the Internet, and where messages are stored until their recipients connect to the Internet to collect their email.

MAILBOX
The area on a mail server used to store email messages for a particular email address.

MODEM
A device used to connect to the Internet over a telephone line.

NETWORK
A collection of computers that are linked together.

NEWS SERVER
A large computer used to relay newsgroup messages over the newsgroup network, Usenet.

NEWSGROUP
A discussion group on the Internet where people exchange news, views, and other kinds of information.

OFFLINE
Not Connected to the Internet.

ONLINE
Connected to the Internet.

OUTBOX
The folder in which Outlook Express stores sent email messages.

PAPERCLIP ICON
When this icon appears next to a message, it indicates that the message has one or more files attached to it.

PREVIEW PANE
Part of the Outlook Express window that lets you view the contents of a message without opening it in another window.

PRIORITY LEVELS
Any email, either sent or received, can be given a priority level to indicate its importance.

SERVICE PROVIDER
See Internet Service Provider.

TOOLBAR
The row of large buttons along the top of the Outlook Express window that provide shortcuts to the most common operations.

WEB SERVER
A computer with a high-speed connection to the Internet that "serves up" Web pages.

WEB SITE
A collection of Web pages that are linked together in a "web."

WORLD WIDE WEB
The term used to refer to all the Web sites on the Internet that are linked together to form a global "web" of information.

INDEX

ACKNOWLEDGMENTS

PUBLISHER'S ACKNOWLEDGMENTS
Dorling Kindersley would like to thank the following:
Paul Mattock of APM, Brighton, for commissioned photography.
Microsoft Corporation for permission to reproduce screens
from within Microsoft® Outlook® Express.

Every effort has been made to trace the copyright holders.
The publisher apologizes for any unintentional omissions and would be pleased,
in such cases, to place an acknowledgment in future editions of this book.

Microsoft® and Outlook® are registered trademarks of
Microsoft Corporation in the United States and/or other countries.